JOURNEYS

Reader's Notebook
Volume 2

Grade 1

Houghton Mifflin Harcourt

Contents

Lesson 16
READER'S NOTEBOOK

Let's Go to the Moon!
Phonics: Words with Long *o*

Words with Long *o*

 Read the word. Circle the picture that matches the word.

1.

home

2.

go

3.

stone

4.

robe

5.

hole

Words to Know

🖉 Listen to the clues and read along.
Circle the best answer to each clue.

1. This means **in a circle**.   around   think

2. This means **not heavy**.   because   light

3. You do this to let people look
at something.   bring   show

4. After is its opposite.   before   carry

5. You do this with bags.   carry   because

6. This tells why.   because   around

7. Take away is its opposite.   light   bring

8. Your brain does this.   think   before

Words with Long *o*

✏️ Look at the picture. Name each picture.
Write the missing letters to complete the word.

1.

p _ _ l _

2.

b _ _ n _

3.

g _ _ _

4.

r _ p _

5.

s t _ v _

6.

r _ b _

Spelling Words with the Long *o* Sound

Let's Go to the Moon!
Spelling: Words with Long *o*

✏️ Sort the words. Write the correct Spelling Words in each column.

Ends with **o**	Ends with Silent **e**

Spelling Words

so
go
home
hole
no
rope
joke
bone
stove
poke

What Is a Question?

 Circle each question.

1. What did you see?

2. Can you look up?

3. Is that the sun?

4. I think I will read.

5. Where did Mike go?

6. They are at the game.

7. How many rocks does Liz have?

8. I like to tell jokes.

Choose one question. Add details.

_____

_____

_____

_____

Name _____

Using Details

✏️ Draw a picture of something you discovered, or <u>found</u>.

```
┌ ─ ─ ─ ─ ─ ─ ─ ─ ─ ─ ─ ─ ─ ─ ─ ─ ┐
│                                 │
│                                 │
│                                 │
│                                 │
└ ─ ─ ─ ─ ─ ─ ─ ─ ─ ─ ─ ─ ─ ─ ─ ─ ┘
```

✏️ Write sentences about when you <u>saw</u> your discovery.

_____

One day I **found** a _____ .

_____

When I **saw** it, I _____

_____

Then I _____ .

Main Idea

_____

All my sentences tell about _____ .

Name _____

Words with Long *u*

 Circle the word that names the picture.

1.

flute   flat

2.

mole   mule

3.

hang   huge

4.

cute   cut

5.

cone   cube

Phonics

7

Grade 1, Unit 4

Name _____   Date _____

Reader's Guide

Let's Go to the Moon!

Interview an Astronaut

Today you are a reporter. A reporter asks a person questions and writes down the answers. Read pages 20–23. Think about what you read. Then write a question you would like to ask an astronaut. Then pretend to be the astronaut. Write the answer.

Q:

A:

Name _____ Date _____

Read pages 28–33. Think about what you
read. Write a question you would like to ask
an astronaut. Then pretend to be the astronaut.
Write your answer.

Q: _____

_____

_____

A: _____

_____

_____

_____

_____

_____

_____

Spelling Words with the Long *o* Sound

Spelling Words

so
go
home
hole
no
rope
joke
bone
stove
poke

✏️ Write the Spelling Words that rhyme with **woke.**

_____ _____

1. _____ 2. _____

✏️ Write the Spelling Words that begin with **h.**

_____ _____

3. _____ 4. _____

✏️ Write the Spelling Words that rhyme with **Jo.**

_____

5. _____

_____

6. _____

_____

7. _____

Name _____

Lesson 16
READER'S NOTEBOOK

Let's Go to the Moon!
Grammar: Questions

Writing Questions

Write the correct word from the Word Bank to begin each sentence. Write the correct end mark.

Word Bank

What	Can	When	Where	Do	Are

1. _____ can I put my hat ____

2. _____ can they see ____

3. _____ you see me ____

4. _____ you need a snack ____

5. _____ you cold ____

6. _____ do you go ____

Planning My Sentences

 Draw and write details that tell what happened.

_____

- -

My Topic: _____

First Detail

↓

Second Detail

↓

Last Detail

Name _____

Lesson 16
READER'S NOTEBOOK

Let's Go to the Moon!
Spelling: Words with Long *o*

Spelling Words with the Long *o* Sound

 Write a Spelling Word to complete each sentence.

Spelling Words

so
go
home
hole
no
rope
joke
bone
stove
poke

1. The pot on the _____ is hot.

2. Can you wrap the _____ around the pole?

3. What _____ does a fox live in?

4. I can tell a funny _____ .

5. Stand up _____ that I can see you.

6. It is time to _____ to bed.

13
Grade 1, Unit 4

Spiral Review

✏️ Circle each proper noun. Some of them have two words in their name. Then write the proper noun correctly.

1. My friend mel has a box
   of gem stones.

   _____
   _____
   _____

2. We live in oak lane.

   _____
   _____

3. She has a cat named red.

   _____
   _____

4. I saw the dog show.

   _____

✏️ Draw a line under each title. Then write the titles and names correctly.

5. Mom's friend is mrs. Dell.

   _____
   _____

6. Will dr. Wade visit the class?

   _____

Name _____

Lesson 16
READER'S NOTEBOOK

Let's Go to the Moon!
Grammar: Questions

Grammar in Writing

A sentence that asks something is called a **question.** A question begins with a capital letter and ends with a **question mark.**

✏️ **Fix the mistakes in these sentences. Use proofreading marks.**

Examples: <u>d</u>oes the moon have plants?∧

Is the moon dusty?∧

1. Did you know his name

2. when did they go?

3. Why do you have your bike.

4. what do cats eat?

5. is the Moon hot or cold.

Proofreading Marks	
∧	Add
≡	Capital letter

Words with Long *e*

✏️ Circle the word that matches the picture.

1.

feel   feet

2.

tree   tea

3.

me   he

4.

leaf   leap

5.

seat   street

6.

see   bee

Name _____

Words to Know

Listen to the questions. Read along.
Circle the best answer to each question.

1. What word goes with **might**? maybe   there

2. What word goes with **do not**? car   don't

3. What word goes with **true**? could   sure

4. What word goes with **drive**? car   there

5. What word goes with **here**? there   don't

6. What word goes with **can**? cart   could

7. What word comes after the
   words "**This story is** _____"? don't   about

8. What word tells how you travel? by   maybe

Name _____

Lesson 17
READER'S NOTEBOOK

Words with Long *e*

The Big Trip
Phonics: Words with Long *e*

Circle the word that completes the sentence.

1. I can _____ you how to plant seeds.

    teach   **beach**

2. These are big _____ .

    bees   **seeds**

3. I will put them in _____ holes.

    jeep   **deep**

4. Help me _____ my watering can.

    reach   **peach**

5. Before long, we will see a small _____ .

    beef   **leaf**

The Big Trip
Spelling: Words with Long *e*

Spelling Words with the Long *e* Sound

Sort the words. Write the correct Spelling Words in each column.

Spelling Words

me
be
read
feet
tree
keep
eat
mean
sea
these

Words with e	Words with ea	Words with ee
_____	_____	_____
_____	_____	_____
_____	_____	_____
_____	_____	_____
_____	_____	_____
_____	_____	_____
_____	_____	_____
_____	_____	_____

Word with Silent e

_____

Compound Sentences

✏️ Draw a line under the correct compound sentence in each pair.

1. Max took the bus, and we walked.

   Max took the bus and we walked.

2. Do you know, or should I tell you.

   Do you know, or should I tell you?

3. Work quickly, but be careful.

   Work quickly, but be careful?

✏️ Write the correct end mark to finish each compound sentence.

____

4. Stay in line, and wait for the bell ____

5. Is your sister here, or is she at home ____

Details for Where and When

 Draw a picture of something you saw or did on a trip.

Write sentences about your trip.

Who	Action	Where

Who	Action	When

Who	Action	Where

Words Ending with *ng, nk*

 Circle the letters that finish the word.
Write the word.

1.

ba____

(nk,   ng)

_____

- - - - - - - - - - - -

_____

2.

dri____

(nk,   ng)

_____

- - - - - - - - - - - -

_____

3.

swi____

(nk,   ng)

_____

- - - - - - - - - - - -

_____

4.

ki____

(nk,   ng)

_____

- - - - - - - - - - - -

_____

The Big Trip

Travel Riddles

Let's have fun with riddles about **The Big Trip**! Read the clues and the question. Write the answer in a sentence.

I have two wheels. I am pulled by an animal. What am I? *Do you need a clue? Read pages 60–61.*

_____

- -

_____.

I have no wheels. You can ride in my basket. I go in the air. What am I? *Do you need a clue? Read pages 64–65.*

_____

- -

_____.

I have four wheels. You can put your suitcase on top of me. What am I? *Do you need a clue? Read pages 56–57.*

_____

- -

_____.

Name _____ Date _____

Now you write a travel riddle! After you write your riddle, share it with a friend. A riddle gives clues. You write the clues. Then a riddle asks a question. The question is already written. You write the answer. Do not let your friend see it! Write the pages from **The Big Trip** where your reader can find clues.

_____
- - - - - - - - - - - - - - - - - -
Clues: _____
_____
- - - - - - - - - - - - - - - - - -
_____
_____
- - - - - - - - - - - - - - - - - -
_____
                          _____
                          - - - - - - - -
What kind of travel am I? _____
Do you need a clue? Read pages:
_____
- - - - - - - - - - - - - - - - - -
_____

Name _____

Spelling Words with the Long *e* Sound

 Write the Spelling Word that names each picture.

me

be

read

feet

tree

keep

eat

mean

sea

these

1. _____

2. _____

3. _____

4. _____

5. _____

6. _____

Spelling

Grade 1, Unit 4

Lesson 17
READER'S NOTEBOOK

The Big Trip
Grammar: Compound Sentences

Writing Compound Sentences

Write a compound sentence by combining each pair of shorter sentences.

1. Are you ready?   Should I wait?

_____

_ or

_____

_ _

2. Walk the dog.   Feed the cat.

_____

_ _ _ _ _ _ _ _ _ _ _ _ _ _ _ _ _ and

_____

_ _

3. I feel good.   Joe is sick.

_____

_ _ _ _ _ _ _ _ _ _ _ _ _ _ _ _ _ but

_____

_ _

Name _____

Lesson 17
READER'S NOTEBOOK

Planning My Sentences

The Big Trip
Writing: Narrative Writing

✏️ Draw and write details that tell what happened first, next, and last.

_____

- - - - - - - - - - - - - - - - - -

My Topic: _____

First

↓

Next

↓

Last

Spelling Words with the Long e Sound

✎ Write a Spelling Word from the box to complete each sentence.

Spelling Words

me

be

read

feet

tree

keep

eat

mean

sea

these

1. Look at the leaves on that

_____

- - - - - - - - - - - - - - - -

_____ .

2. What do you _____ in

your backpack?

3. I like to swim in the _____ .

4. Pick from _____ games.

5. A duck has two _____ .

6. Will you _____ to me?

Spiral Review

 Draw a line under each command.

1. We watched the game.

2. Watch where you walk.

3. Be kind to the animals.

4. What kind of dog is that?

 Add words to each command to make a compound sentence.

5. Wait for your turn.

_____

- -

_____

- -

_____

6. Listen carefully.

_____

- -

_____

- -

_____

Grammar in Writing

A **compound sentence** is made up of two shorter sentences joined by a comma and **and**, **but**, or **or**.

Underline each compound sentence.

1. The girls walked or rode the bus to school.

2. Mom drives to work, but Dad takes a train.

3. Is the game today, or is it tomorrow?

Write a compound sentence by combining the two shorter sentences.

4. Take a nap.   Don't be late.

_____ but _

_____

5. I have paper.   Larry has pencils.

_____

_____ and _

_____

Name _____

Words with *ai*, *ay*

✏️ Read the words. Circle the word that names the picture. Then write the word.

1.

tray   ray

_____
- - - - - - - - - - - - - - - - - -
_____

2.

sail   nail

_____
- - - - - - - - - - - - - - - - - -
_____

3.

hay   day

_____
- - - - - - - - - - - - - - - - - -
_____

4.

paint   pain

_____
- - - - - - - - - - - - - - - - - -
_____

5.

train   rain

_____
- - - - - - - - - - - - - - - - - -
_____

Words to Know

Circle the correct word to complete
each sentence.

1. Fran ate her beets (these, first).

2. Beets are planted in the (ground, sometimes).

3. (Food, Sometimes) Fran eats salad, too.

4. Fran has to eat all the (food, your) on her plate.

5. "Eat (ground, your) peas," said Mom.

6. The peas are (your, right) from the shop.

7. Fran looked (under, first) her peas.

8. Fran said, "(These, Under) peas look good!"

Words with *ai*, *ay*

✏️ **Read the words. Circle the word that names the picture.**

1.

tray   ray

2.

sail   tail

3.

may   play

4.

rain   main

5.

paint   pant

Lesson 18
READER'S NOTEBOOK

Where Does Food Come From?
Spelling: Words with *ai, ay*

Spelling Words with the Vowel Pairs *ai, ay*

✏️ Sort the words. Write the correct Spelling Words in each column.

Words with **ai**	Words with **ay**
_____	_____
_____	_____
_____	_____
_____	_____
_____	_____
_____	_____
_____	_____
_____	_____
_____	_____
_____	_____
_____	_____

Spelling Words

play
grain
sail
mail
may
rain
way
day
stay
pain

Months, Days, and Holidays

✏️ Listen to the names in the Word Bank. Read along. Circle the month, day, or holiday in each sentence. Write it correctly on the line.

Word Bank

Labor Day	Tuesday	May	June	Saturday	August

_____

1. On labor day we had a picnic. _____

_____

2. On tuesday Hank makes a cake. _____

_____

3. We plant seeds each may. _____

✏️ Draw a line under the correct sentence in each pair.

4. Ike likes June for planting beans.

Ike likes june for planting beans.

5. I picked beans on Saturday.

I picked beans on saturday.

6. Peaches grow best in august.

Peaches grow best in August.

Name _____

Lesson 18
READER'S NOTEBOOK

Where Does Food Come From?
Writing: Narrative Writing

Using Different Kinds of Sentences

✏️ Write a friendly letter about a special meal you had. Write statements and a question.

20

Dear _____,

_____

I ate _____ with _____.

_____

_____

(statement)

_____

_____

(statement)

_____

_____?

(question)

_____

_____,

_____

Name _____

Contractions 'll, 'd

 Write a word from the box to finish each sentence.

I would   I'd

| he'd | she'll | I'd | they'll | we'd |

_____

1. Ben said that _____ be late today.

_____

2. Beth said _____ go to the beach.

_____

3. Mom and Dad said _____ go out at five.

_____

4. Gus said, "_____ like to play in the sand."

_____

5. We think _____ like a day at the beach.

Name _____ Date _____

Lesson 18
READER'S NOTEBOOK

Where Does Food
Come From?
Independent Reading

Where Does Food Come From?

Make a Meal!

I am going to have a glass of milk and a grilled cheese sandwich with tomatoes for lunch. I need four different kinds of food. Write where each food comes from. Look at pages 98–99, 104–105, and 107 for text evidence to help you.

1. Milk comes from

_____

- -

_____ .

2. Bread comes from

_____

- -

_____ .

3. Cheese comes from

_____

- -

_____ .

4. Tomatoes come from

_____

- -

_____ .

Now it's time for breakfast! Draw foods on the plate. Label them. Write a sentence telling where each food comes from. Look in the selection for text evidence to help you.

_____

- -

_____

_____

- -

_____

_____

- -

_____

Lesson 18
READER'S NOTEBOOK

Spelling Words with the Vowel Pairs *ai*, *ay*

Where Does Food Come From?
Spelling: Words with *ai, ay*

✏️ Write the Spelling Words that rhyme with **fail.**

Spelling Words

play
grain
sail
mail
may
rain
way
day
stay
pain

_____   _____

1. _____   2. _____

✏️ Write the Spelling Words that rhyme with **bay.**

_____   _____

3. _____   4. _____

_____   _____

5. _____   6. _____

_____

7. _____

✏️ Write the Spelling Words that rhyme with **main.**

_____   _____   _____

8. _____   9. _____   10. _____

Commas in Dates

 Circle the comma in each date.

1. Ms. Ray moved to the farm on October 25, 2016.

2. She planted wheat on March 13, 2017.

3. She got some chicks on May 28, 2017.

4. She had eggs for sale on June 4, 2018.

 The date in each sentence is underlined.
Write the date correctly.

5. This patch was planted on <u>march 16 2018</u>.

_____

- -

_____

6. The peas were planted on <u>april 23 2018</u>.

_____

- -

_____

Planning My Letter

 Write and draw details that tell what happened first, next, and last.

I will write my letter to _____ .

I will tell about _____ .

First

↓

Next

↓

Last

Spelling Words with the Long *a* Sound

✏️ **Write the correct word to complete each sentence.**

_____

_ _ _ _ _ _ _ _ _ _ _ _ _ _ _ _ _ _

1. Can you come out and _____ ?

play   clay

_____

_ _ _ _ _ _ _ _ _ _ _ _ _ _ _ _ _ _

2. In April there is a lot of _____ .

rake   rain

_____

_ _ _ _ _ _ _ _ _ _ _ _ _ _ _ _ _ _

3. Let us _____ on the lake.

sail   tail

_____

_ _ _ _ _ _ _ _ _ _ _ _ _ _ _ _ _ _

4. I feel a _____ in my leg.

train   pain

_____

_ _ _ _ _ _ _ _ _ _ _ _ _ _ _ _ _ _

5. Wheat is a _____ .

grain   green

Name _____

Spiral Review

✏️ Circle the correct verb. Then write the sentence with the correct verb.

1. The kids (walk, walks) around the pond.

_____

- -

_____

2. Nine sheep (eat, eats) the grass.

_____

- -

_____

3. Ducks (flap, flaps) their wings.

_____

- -

_____

4. One mule (sleep, sleeps) in the hay.

_____

- -

_____

5. Pigs (play, plays) in the mud.

_____

- -

_____

Grammar in Writing

The name of each **month, day,** and **holiday** begins with a capital letter. When you write a date, use a **comma** between the day of the month and the year.

Example:

labor day is monday september 7 2018.

Listen to the names of months and holidays in the Word Bank. Read along. Fix the mistakes in these sentences. Use proofreading marks.

> ### Word Bank
>
> July   August   September   October
>
> December   New Year's Eve

1. In october it was cold.

2. Mr. Potts left on august 22 2018.

3. Every september they sell jam.

4. Ms. Down opened the shop on july 18 2018.

5. new year's eve is on december 31.

Proofreading Marks			
∧	Add	≡	Capital letter

Name _____

Words with *oa*, *ow*

 Read the word. Circle the picture that matches the word.

1.

boat

2.

crow

3.

goat

4.

bowl

5.

loaf

Words to Know

✏️ Listen to the clues. Read along. Circle the best answer to each clue.

1. This means **finished**.   paper   done

2. This is in a short while.   soon   great

3. This means **speak**.   were   talk

4. Awful is its opposite.   great   soon

5. A joke makes you do this.   laugh   done

6. You write on this.   work   paper

7. This is a **job**.   great   work

8. Past tense for **are**.   laugh   were

Words with *oa*, *ow*

✏️ Circle the two words in each row that rhyme. Then write the letters that stand for the long **o** sound.

1.

grow   blow   block   gray   ___ ___

2.

slow   sling   throw   thick   ___ ___

3.

much   road   load   lunch   ___ ___

4.

coat   got   goat   long   ___ ___

5.

flame   show   ground   snow   ___ ___

Tomás Rivera
Spelling: Words with *oa, ow*

Name _____

Spelling Words with Vowel Pairs *oa*, *ow*

Sort the words. Write the correct Spelling Words in each column.

Spelling Words

show
row
boat
blow
toad
road
low
coat
grow
snow

Words with **ow**	Words with **oa**

Future Using *will*

✏️ Circle the sentences that tell about the future. Rewrite the other sentences to tell about the future using *will*.

1. I read each day.

2. Brent will meet you at the shop.

3. My dad helps me read.

4. They washed the van.

5. Fran will beat the eggs.

_____

6. _____

_____

7. _____

_____

8. _____

_____

Order of Events

 Draw pictures to show what you did to get ready for school today.

 Write sentences about what you did to get ready for school today.

_____

First, _____

_____

Next, _____

_____

Last, _____

Contractions 've, 're

 Draw a line from each pair of words to its contraction.

You are	You're
They have	I've
I have	We're
We are	They've

✏️ Write a sentence using one of the contractions from above.

_____

- -

_____

- -

_____

Contractions *'ve, 're*

 Write the contraction that finishes each sentence.

_____

----

1. _____ all set for our big game.

   We   are

   _____

   ----

2. _____ my best friend.

   You   are

   _____

   ----

3. _____ had a lot of fun today!

   I   have

   _____

   ----

4. _____ had a lot of rain.

   They   have

Tomás Rivera

Introducing Tomás Rivera

Let's make a sign for the Tomás Rivera Library!

Read pages 134–138. Tell people what was important to Tomás Rivera. Tell why the library has his name.

The Tomás Rivera Library

_____

- -

_____

- -

_____

- -

_____

- -

_____

- -

_____

Read pages 139–141. Draw something
that was important to Tomás Rivera.
Write a caption for your drawing to tell why
it was important.

_____

- -

_____

_____

- -

_____

_____

- -

Spelling Words with Vowel Pairs *oa*, *ow*

Write the Spelling Word that fits each clue.

Spelling Words

show
row
grow
low
blow
snow
boat
coat
road
toad

1. Opposite of **high**

2. Another word for **street**

3. You watch this on TV.

4. You see this in winter.

5. Wear this in the cold.

6. An animal

Future Using *going to*

Circle the sentences that tell about the future. Rewrite the other sentences to tell about the future. Use **going to** in each one.

1. I work with Ed.

2. Ed is going to have many crops.

3. My dad planted beets.

4. They pulled the weeds.

5. Jen is going to pick beans with Sam.

6. Tess has a pet cat.

7. _____

8. _____

9. _____

10. _____

Spelling Words with the Long *o* Sound

✏️ Write the correct word to complete each sentence.

_____

1. The class will put on a _____.

   show   snow

_____

2. The _____ hopped on the grass.

   toad   load

_____

3. How do plants _____?

   throw   grow

_____

4. The _____ came in with fish.

   boat   bat

_____

5. Which _____ will you sit in?

   row   read

Spiral Review

✏️ Notice the clue word **yesterday** that tells about the past. Circle the verb that tells about the past. Then write those verbs.

1. **Yesterday** mom (works, worked) at the new shop.

2. She (opens, opened) the shop at nine.

3. Many kids (walk, walked) into the shop.

4. Val (asks, asked) for a new game.

5. Her mom (helps, helped) her.

Name _____

Planning My Personal Narrative

✏️ Draw and write details that tell what happened first, next, and last.

_____

_ _

My Topic: _____

First

Next

Last

Grammar in Writing

You can write sentences that tell what may happen in the future. Use **will** or **is going to** to write sentences about the future.

Example: Jill walks.

Jill **will** walk.

Jill **is going to** walk.

Rewrite each sentence to tell about the future.

1. Tom runs far.

_____

- -

_____

2. He went to work.

_____

- -

_____

3. Grandpa sails his boat.

_____

- -

_____

- -

_____

Compound Words

✏️ Name each picture. Circle two words to make a compound for the picture. Write the compound word.

1.

    sea   pea   _____

    nut   side   _____

2.

    trail   rain   _____

    bow   mix   _____

3.

    blue   sea   _____

    bird   shell   _____

4.

    snow   mail   _____

    box   flake   _____

5.

    cup   sail   _____

    cake   boat   _____

Words to Know

 Circle the best answer to each question.

1. What word goes with **less**?   more   use

2. What word goes with **dry**?   door   wash

3. What word goes with **open**?   want   door

4. What word goes with **father**?   mother   more

5. What word goes with **new**?   old   wash

6. What word goes with **need**?   wash   want

7. What word goes with **test**?   more   try

8. What word goes with **tools**?   use   mother

Name _____

Compound Words

Choose words from the box to make a compound word to name each picture. Write the word. You will use some words more than once.

mail	rain	sail	sand	bow
row	boat	coat	box	

1.

_____

2.

_____

3.

_____

4.

_____

5.

_____

6.

_____

Spelling Compound Words

Write the two words that make up each Spelling Word shown below.

1. bedtime

2. himself

3. flagpole

4. sailboat

5. backpack

6. sunset

7. raincoat

Name _____

Lesson 20
READER'S NOTEBOOK

Little Rabbit's Tale
Grammar: Prepositions

Prepositional Phrases for Where

✏ Circle the prepositional phase in each sentence. Write it on the line.

1. Rabbit went to Squirrel's home.

_____

- -

_____

2. He went up the steps.

_____

- -

_____

3. He knocked on the door.

_____

- -

_____

Complete each sentence. Write a prepositional phrase that tells where.

_____

- -

4. The rabbit lives _____ .

_____

- -

5. The rabbit hopped _____ .

Name _____

Exact Details

✏️ Read each underlined detail. Write a more exact detail to finish each sentence.

1. I watched <u>an animal</u>.

_____

I watched _____ .

2. I fed it <u>some food</u>.

_____

I fed it _____ .

3. It <u>moved around</u>.

_____

It _____ .

4. I will teach it <u>something</u>.

_____

I will teach it _____ .

Writing   **67**   Grade 1, Unit 4

Words with Short Vowel /ĕ/*ea*

 Circle two words that have the short
e sound.

_____

1.

red   bread   bat   rode

_____

2.

sled   bone   robe   head

_____

3.

bed   dead   cube   lot

_____

4.

peach   fed   Fred   drink

_____

5.

led   paint   loaf   thread

_____

Reader's Guide

Little Rabbit's Tale

Goose and Beaver Tell the Tale

It is time for Goose and Beaver to tell the story!

Read pages 164–169. Tell this part of the story the way Goose would tell it. Tell how Goose feels and what happens.

Name _____ Date _____

Read pages 174–179. Tell the end of the
story like Beaver would tell it. Why is
Beaver unhappy at Little Rabbit's house?
What happens next?

Spelling Compound Words

🖊 Draw a line from a word on the left to a word on the right to make each Spelling Word.

1. bath   time
2. flag   tub
3. bed   pole
4. sun   pack
5. back   set
6. play   coat
7. rain   pen
8. sail   side
9. in   self
10. him   boat

Spelling Words

bedtime
sunset
bathtub
sailboat
flagpole
backpack
playpen
raincoat
inside
himself

Prepositional Phrases

Circle the prepositional phrase in each sentence. Decide if the prepositional phrase tells where or when. Write **where** or **when** on the line.

_____

1. The friends play after lunch.

_____

2. They meet at Viv's home.

_____

3. Viv swings under a tree.

_____

4. Lin skips on the grass.

_____

5. Mom comes home at five o'clock.

_____

6. Lin goes home before then.

_____

Lesson 20
READER'S NOTEBOOK

Little Rabbit's Tale
Spelling: Compound Words

Spelling Compound Words

✏️ **Write the correct word to complete each sentence.**

_____

- -

1. The _____ was very red.

   sunset   himself

   _____

   -

2. Let us play _____ today.

   inside   flagpole

   _____

   -

3. I carry my _____ with me.

   playpen   backpack

   _____

   -

4. Before _____ I brush my teeth.

   bedtime   sailboat

   _____

   -

5. My _____ has a matching hat.

   bathtub   raincoat

Spiral Review

 Write each sentence with the correct verb.

1. This puppet (is, are) small.

_____

- -

_____

2. Raindrops (is, are) wet.

_____

- -

_____

3. The lambs (is, are) white.

_____

- -

_____

4. The show (was, were) funny.

_____

- -

_____

5. Those muffins (was, were) huge.

_____

- -

_____

Grammar in Writing

A prepositional phrase can tell when or where.

> Example: We walk **after lunch**.   when
>
> We walk **in the park**.   where

✎ Add a prepositional phrase to each sentence to tell when or where. Write the new sentence on the line.

1. My friends and I ran.

_____

- -

_____

2. Something fell.

_____

- -

_____

3. I tripped.

_____

- -

_____

4. I went home.

_____

- -

_____

Amazing Whales!

What I Know About Whales

Draw your favorite whale. Label your picture.
Tell one fact that makes this whale amazing.

Kind of whale

_____

- -

Amazing Fact

_____

- -

Whales are in trouble! Write three things people can do to help them.

1. _____

2. _____

3. _____

Words with *ar*

✏️ Circle the word that matches the picture.

1.

cat   card

2.

star   stamp

3.

march   much

4.

barn   bark

5.

arm   art

6.

yard   yarn

Words to Know

✏️ Circle the correct word to complete each sentence.

1. Dad reads us a funny (story, noise).

2. The children are making a lot of (loudly, noise).

3. Tim's parents are planning a trip around the (world, window).

4. Those children are talking (loudly, story) in class.

5. I (few, shall) be late for school tomorrow.

6. Some animals hunt at (night, world).

7. Close your (night, window) when it rains.

8. (Few, Shall) birds can swim.

Words with *ar*

Look at the picture and read the words.
Write the word that matches the picture.

1.

stem   start

_____

- - - - - - - - - - - - -

_____

2.

cat   cart

_____

- - - - - - - - - - - - -

_____

3.

car   card

_____

- - - - - - - - - - - - -

_____

4.

shake   shark

_____

- - - - - - - - - - - - -

_____

5.

pack   park

_____

- - - - - - - - - - - - -

_____

Spelling Words with *r*-Controlled Vowel *ar*

Spelling Words

far
arm
yard
art
jar
bar
barn
bark
card
yarn

 Write the Spelling Words that rhyme with **far**, **yard**, and **barn**.

_____

1. **Far** rhymes with _____

_____

and _____ .

_____

2. **Yard** rhymes with _____ .

_____

_____

3. **Barn** rhymes with _____ .

Write the Spelling Word that names the picture.

4.

_____

5.

_____

6.

_____

Pronouns That Name One

✏️ Circle the pronoun that can take the place of the underlined word or words.

1. <u>Grandpa</u> makes a shed.

    He   She   It

2. <u>The shed</u> is short and wide.

    He   She   It

3. <u>Ann</u> helps Grandpa work in the shed.

    He   She   It

✏️ Write **He**, **She**, or **It** to take the place of the underlined word or words.

4. <u>Joe</u> sees a nest.

_____

_____ sees a nest.

5. <u>The nest</u> has eggs.

_____

_____ has eggs.

82

Dialogue

🖊 Think of another problem that Toad could have with his garden. Then write what he and Frog might have said.

Toad still needed help with his garden. He asked Frog what

" _____

- -

to do. _____

_____

- -

_____ ?" Toad asked.

" _____

- -

_____

- -

_____ ," said Frog.

Words with *or*, *ore*

Read the sentences. Circle the sentence
that tells about the picture.

1. We look at the score.

We look at the star.

2. I like to do chores.

I snore when I sleep.

3. She finds shells at the shore.

She finds fish at the shop.

4. He can play the thorn.

He can play the horn.

5. Here is a jar.

Here is a fork.

Reader's Guide

The Garden

Could That Really Happen?

Think about the story and what could happen in real life.

Read pages 15–18. Read what happens. Decide if it could happen in real life. Tell why or why not.

What Happens	Could this happen in real life? Why or why not?
A frog and toad talk to each other.	
The seeds did not grow right after they were put in the ground.	

Read pages 19–29. Fill in the chart.

What Happens	Could this happen in real life? Why or why not?
Frog said that shouting at the seeds kept them from growing.	
The seeds were afraid of the dark.	
Letting the sun shine on the seeds and the rain fall on them helped them grow.	

Spelling Words with r-Controlled Vowel *ar*

✏️ Write the Spelling Word that names the picture.

Spelling Words

far
arm
yard
art
jar
bar
barn
bark
card
yarn

1.

_____

2.

_____

3.

_____

4.

_____

5.

_____

6.

_____

Pronouns That Name More Than One

Circle the pronoun that can take the place of each underlined subject.

1. <u>Workers</u> plant trees in the park.

   We   They

2. <u>The trees</u> grow big.

   We   They

3. <u>Sis and I</u> sit under the trees.

   We   They

Write **We** or **They** to take the place of each underlined subject.

4. <u>Dad and I</u> walk to the park.

   - - - - - - - - - - - - - - - - - -

   _____ walk to the park.

5. <u>Pete and Kate</u> run and play.

   - - - - - - - - - - - - - - - - - -

   _____ run and play.

Planning My Sentences

Write and draw details that tell what happened first and next.

Topic: After Toad's garden started to grow,

_____

– –

Frog and Toad _____ .

First	

↓

Next	

Spelling Words with r-Controlled Vowel *ar*

Write the correct word to complete each sentence.

1. She lives _____ away from me.

| fun | far |

2. He waves his _____ in the air.

| ants | arm |

3. We play in the _____ .

| yard | yarn |

4. We paint in _____ class.

| art | part |

5. She gave me a _____ of jam.

| bar | jar |

6. Hang your coats on the _____ .

| card | bar |

7. The sheep are in the _____ .

| barn | big |

Spiral Review

 Draw a line under each question.

1. What sort of tree is this?

2. Do all trees have leaves?

3. Pine trees have cones.

4. What animals live in trees?

5. Birds live in trees.

6. Do we need trees?

7. Trees give us air.

8. Do we get food from trees?

Grammar in Writing

The pronouns **he, she,** and **it** name one. The pronouns **we** and **they** name more than one.

🖉 **Fix the mistakes in the sentences. Use proofreading marks.**

Example: The shed is done. ~~She~~ looks nice.
                                                         It
                                                         ∧

1. Mom saws. He makes a shelf for the shed.

2. Bob and I get paint. They paint the shelf.

3. Mom has some grapes. It puts them in a bowl.

4. My friends come over. We want to see the shed.

Proofreading Marks	
∧	add
⤴	take out

Words with *er*, *ir*, *ur*

Amazing Animals
Phonics: *r*-Controlled Vowels
er, ir, ur

✏ Read the word. Circle the picture that matches the word.

1.	bird		
2.	turn		
3.	her		
4.	burn		
5.	third		
6.	herd		

Words to Know

Circle the word that best completes each sentence.

1. I like (until, learning) about animals.

2. Our dog Pip is five (follow, years) old.

3. Pip has (baby, eight) new pups.

4. She will feed her pups (until, learning) they are older.

5. A (eight, young) kitten came to our home.

6. The new kitten likes to (until, follow) Pip.

7. The kitten (begins, learning) to think he is Pip's pup!

8. The new kitten is not Pip's (years, baby).

Words with *er*, *ir*, *ur*

✏️ Read the words in the box. Write the word that matches the picture.

clerk	shirt	stir	hurt	curl

1. _____

2. _____

3. _____

4. _____

5. _____

Spelling Words with *r*-Controlled Vowels *er*, *ir*, *ur*

 Write the Spelling Words with **er**.

_____   _____
- - - - - - - - - - - - - - - - - -   - - - - - - - - - - - - - - - - - -
1. _____   2. _____

 Write the Spelling Words with **ir**.

_____   _____
- - - - - - - - - - - - - - - - - -   - - - - - - - - - - - - - - - - - -
3. _____   4. _____

_____   _____
- - - - - - - - - - - - - - - - - -   - - - - - - - - - - - - - - - - - -
5. _____   6. _____

_____
- - - - - - - - - - - - - - - - - -
7. _____

 Write the Spelling Words with **ur**.

_____   _____
- - - - - - - - - - - - - - - - - -   - - - - - - - - - - - - - - - - - -
8. _____   9. _____

_____
- - - - - - - - - - - - - - - - - -
10. _____

Spelling Words

sir
fern
girl
her
third
hurt
fur
bird
turn
stir

Name _____

Lesson 22
READER'S NOTEBOOK

Amazing Animals
Grammar: The Pronouns
I and *Me*

Naming Yourself Last

✏️ **Circle the correct words to finish each sentence.**

1. _____ see the goat.

   Jean and me   **Jean and I**

2. Dad took _____ to the zoo.

   I and Steve   **Steve and me**

3. _____ look at the ducks.

   Rex and I   **Rex and me**

✏️ **Write the words from the word box to finish the sentence.**

| Ann   I |

_____   _____

- - - - - - - - - - - - - -   - - - - - - - - - - - - - -

4. _____ and _____

hold the baby snakes.

Exact Verbs

✏️ Draw a picture of an animal for a story. Give your animal a name.

```
Name: _____
```

✏️ Finish these story sentences about your animal. Use exact verbs.

_____ is a _____ .
      name   kind of animal

_____ likes to _____ .
      name   exact verb

_____ always _____ a lot!
      name   exact verb

Name _____

Words with *er*, *ir*, *ur*

✏️ Choose a word from the box to name each picture. Write the word.

girl	turn	chirp	third	hers	dirt

1.

_____
- - - - - - - - -
_____

2.

_____
- - - - - - - - -
_____

3.

_____
- - - - - - - - -
_____

4.

_____
- - - - - - - - -
_____

5.

_____
- - - - - - - - -
_____

6.

_____
- - - - - - - - -
_____

Amazing Animals

Where Is My Home?

The animals got mixed up! Write where each animal lives. Then, write the clues you used to figure out the answer.

pond	ocean	arctic	desert	grassland

Read pages 48–50.

Where is the bear's home? _____

What clues did you use?

_____

- -

_____

Read pages 51–54. Where

is the camel's home? _____

What clues did you use?

_____

- -

_____

Lesson 22
READER'S NOTEBOOK

Amazing Animals
Independent Reading

Read pages 55–56.

Where is the duck's home? _____

What clues did you use?

_____

- -

_____

Read pages 57–58.

Where is the

giraffe's home?

What clues did you use?

_____

- -

_____

Read pages 59–65.

Where is the dolphin's

home? What clues did you use?

_____

- -

_____

Spelling Words with *r*-Controlled Vowels *er*, *ir*, *ur*

Spelling Words

her
fern
girl
sir
stir
bird
fur
hurt
turn
third

 Write the Spelling Word that fits each clue.

_____

1. Opposite of **boy**

_____

2. Goes with **pain**

_____

3. What a bear has

_____

4. Goes with **three**

_____

5. Opposite of **him**

_____

6. An animal

_____

Name _____

Lesson 22
READER'S NOTEBOOK

Naming Yourself with *I*

 Write the sentences correctly.

1. Jay and me visit a farm.

_____

- - - - - - - - - - - - - - - - - - - -

_____

2. Me and Bree feed the ducks.

_____

- - - - - - - - - - - - - - - - - - - -

_____

3. Dave and me pet the sheep.

_____

- - - - - - - - - - - - - - - - - - - -

_____

4. Me and Ed see the lambs.

_____

- - - - - - - - - - - - - - - - - - - -

_____

5. Meg and me hold the cat.

_____

- - - - - - - - - - - - - - - - - - - -

_____

Planning My Sentences

✏️ Write and draw details that tell what happened first and next.

My Topic: I will write about a

_____

- -

_____ .

First

Next

This is how my story will end:

Name _____

Spelling Words with *r*-Controlled Vowels *er*, *ir*, *ur*

 Write the Spelling Word that completes each sentence.

Spelling Words

her
fern
stir
fur
hurt
turn
third
girl
sir
bird

_____

1. I like _____ dress.

_____

2. I watered the _____ .

_____

3. The _____ has a pink doll.

_____

4. I fell and _____ my arm.

_____

5. The _____ laid three eggs.

_____

6. The cat has thick _____ .

Spiral Review

✏️ Draw a line under the two shorter sentences in each compound sentence.

1. Can we go to the zoo, or is it too cold?

2. I want to see the ducks, but they want to see the foxes.

3. Sit quietly, and eat your snack.

✏️ Write a compound sentence by combining the two shorter sentences.

4. Dad baked a cake.   We helped him.

_____

- and

_____

- -

_____

Grammar in Writing

Use the pronoun **I** in the subject of a sentence.
Use the pronoun **me** in the predicate of a
sentence. Name yourself last.

🖉 **Fix the mistakes in these sentences. Use
proofreading marks.**

                         Ted   I
Example: ~~Me~~ and ~~Ted~~ see the ducklings.

1. I and Mark feed the pups.

2. Mom helps me and Jon at the zoo.

3. Me and Hing look at the piglets.

4. Kris and i see the baby birds.

Proofreading Marks	
∧	add
ℒ	take out
≡	capital letter

The Vowel Sound *oo* (book)

✏️ Circle the word that matches the picture.

1.

book   hook

2.

book   cook

3.

wool   wood

4.

hook   hood

5.

brook   took

6.

soot   foot

Words to Know

✏️ **Circle the word that best completes each sentence.**

1. We can go to the play (together, boy).

2. The box has (began, nothing) in it.

3. The new (boy, along) is named Dan.

4. Dan and his (together, father) like to fish.

5. My (house, nothing) has a blue door.

6. Jan skipped (house, along) the path.

7. I will sing the song (again, boy).

8. A bell (house, began) to ring.

Words with *oo (book)*

✏️ Circle the sentence that matches the picture.

1. We cook at mealtime.

We look at the time.

2. I see a little brook.

I see a little book.

3. He has a hat made of wool.

He has a box made of wood.

4. Put your coat on a hook.

Put your coat in a hood.

5. Wash off that soot.

Wash off your foot.

Spelling Words with Vowel Digraph *oo*

✏️ Sort the words. Write the correct Spelling Words in each column.

Words with **ook**	Words with **ood**
_____	_____
_____	_____
_____	_____
_____	_____
_____	_____
_____	_____
_____	_____
_____	_____
_____	_____
_____	_____

Spelling Words

look
book
good
hook
brook
took
foot
shook
wood
hood

Using *my*, *your*, *his*, and *her*

✏️ **Write the correct pronoun to finish each sentence.**

_____

- - - - - - - - - - - - - - - - - -

1. I hug _____ dog Mags.

          me   **my**

_____

- - - - - - - - - - - - - - - - - -

2. Mags runs after _____ stick.

          her   **she**

_____

- - - - - - - - - - - - - - - - - -

3. Rick brings _____ dog.

          he   **his**

_____

- - - - - - - - - - - - - - - - - -

4. You can bring _____ dog, too.

          your   **you**

_____

- - - - - - - - - - - - - - - - - -

5. We can play in _____ backyard!

          they   **my**

Order of Events

✏️ Finish the sentences. Give a summary of
the first part of **Whistle for Willie.**

_____

- -

Peter wished _____ .

_____

- -

He tried _____ .

_____

- -

When Peter saw Willie, he _____

_____

- -

_____ .

_____

- -

Then, Willie _____

_____

- -

_____ .

How Many Syllables?

✏️ Read each word. Circle how many syllables it has. Hint: Each time you hear a vowel sound, there is a syllable.

1.

hammer

1   2

2.

doctor

1   2

3.

stood

1   2

4.

rabbit

1   2

5.

mister

1   2

6.

third

1   2

Reader's Guide

Whistle for Willie

Picture Words

Good readers make pictures in their
mind as they read.

**Read pages 83–87. Draw what Peter is doing on
page 86. Write the words that help you picture it.**

Read pages 88–91. Do you see the cat? Write how the cat might describe what it sees and hears Peter doing.

_____

- -

_____

- -

_____

- -

_____

Read pages 92–103. Then look back at pages 96–97. Write how Willie might describe what he sees and hears.

_____

- -

_____

- -

_____

- -

_____

Name _____

Spelling Words with Vowel Digraph *oo*

✏️ Write each group of Spelling Words in ABC order.

look	hood	shook	hook
good	wood	foot	brook
book		took	

_____

- - - - - - - - - - - -

_____

- - - - - - - - - - - -

_____

Spelling Words

look
book
good
hook
brook
took
foot
shook
wood
hood

Name _____

Using *mine*, *yours*, *his*, *hers*, and *theirs*

🖊 Write the correct pronoun to finish each sentence.

1. This mitt is _____ .

    your   **yours**

2. The bat is _____ .

    he   **his**

3. That treat is _____ .

    their   **theirs**

4. This house is _____ .

    my   **mine**

5. That dog is _____ .

    hers   **her**

Name _____

Planning My Summary

Write sentences and draw details for your summary of **Whistle for Willie.**

_____
- -

My Topic: _____

Spelling Words with the *oo* Sound in *book*

🖊 Write the Spelling Words that make sense in each sentence.

Spelling Words
book
look
good
hook
brook
foot
took
shook
wood
hood

_____

- - - - - - - - - - - - - - - - - -

1. Can I _____ at your

_____

- - - - - - - - - - - - - - - - - -

_____ ?

_____

- - - - - - - - - - - - - - - - - -

2. I _____ the

_____

- - - - - - - - - - - - - - - - - -

_____ off his coat.

_____

- - - - - - - - - - - - - - - - - -

3. I put my _____ in the

_____

- - - - - - - - - - - - - - - - - -

_____ .

Spiral Review

Listen to the names of months in the Word Bank. Read along. Write each date correctly.

Word Bank

February   March   August   October   December

1. The pet shop opened on march 13 2015.

_____

_____

2. Lisa got a cat on february 22 2017.

_____

_____

3. My dog had pups on august 1 2017.

_____

_____

4. His dog won a prize on october 25 2018.

_____

_____

5. My dog got a new bowl on december 22 2018.

_____

_____

Grammar in Writing

- Some pronouns show that something belongs to someone.

- The pronouns **my**, **your**, **his**, **her**, and **their** come before a noun.

- The pronouns **mine**, **yours**, **his**, **hers**, and **theirs** come at the end of a sentence.

 Fix the mistakes. Use proofreading marks.

Example: The dog is ~~he.~~ *his*

1. I play with ~~mine~~ dog. (1 point) *my*

2. That is ~~hers~~ bowl. (1) *her*

3. This leash is ~~your.~~ (1) *yours*

4. Jack has a new dog. The dog is ~~hers.~~ (1) *his*

5. The children have pets. The pets are ~~their.~~ (1) *theirs*

Proofreading Marks	
∧	add
⟋○	take out

Read directions to children.

Grammar
© Houghton Mifflin Harcourt Publishing Company. All rights reserved.

122

Assessment Tip: Total 5 points

Grade 1, Unit 5

Words with *oo* (moon), *ou*, *ew*

 Circle the word that names the picture.

1.

moth   moon

2.

spoon   spot

3.

scream   screw

4.

soap   soup

5.

boat   boot

6.

stool   stole

Words to Know

Write a word from the box to complete each sentence.

1. I planted flowers in the _____.

2. Our heater _____ our house.

3. Pete _____ hit a home run.

4. Mr. Lee lives in the _____.

5. Mom _____ us with a blanket.

6. Are you _____ to go?

7. Dinosaurs walked the _____ millions of years ago.

8. I got many _____ of games for my birthday.

Words with *oo* (moon), *ou, ew*

 Write the word that best completes each sentence. Use the words in the Word Bank.

> **Word Bank**
>
> cool   group   room   drew   stool

_____

- - - - - - - - - - - - - - - - - - - -

1. I got together with a _____ of friends.

_____

- - - - - - - - - - - - - - - - - - - -

2. We had fun playing in my _____ .

_____

- - - - - - - - - - - - - - - - - - - -

3. We _____ some pictures and hung them up.

_____

- - - - - - - - - - - - - - - - - - - -

4. Then we painted my old _____ .

_____

- - - - - - - - - - - - - - - - - - - -

5. Now the room looks _____ !

Spelling Words with Vowel Digraphs *oo, ou, ew*

 Write the Spelling Words with **ou**.

_____   _____
- - - - - - - - - - - - -   - - - - - - - - - - - - -
1. _____   2. _____

Write the Spelling Words with **ew**.

_____   _____
- - - - - - - - - - - - -   - - - - - - - - - - - - -
3. _____   4. _____

Write the Spelling Words with **oo**.

_____   _____
- - - - - - - - - - - - -   - - - - - - - - - - - - -
5. _____   6. _____

_____   _____
- - - - - - - - - - - - -   - - - - - - - - - - - - -
7. _____   8. _____

_____   _____
- - - - - - - - - - - - -   - - - - - - - - - - - - -
9. _____   10. _____

Spelling Words

soon
new
noon
zoo
boot
too
moon
blew
soup
you

Indefinite Pronouns

✏️ **Indefinite pronouns** are special **pronouns** that stand for people or things that are not named.

┌─────────────── **Word Bank** ───────────────┐

anyone   someone   everything

something   everybody   somebody

└──┘

✏️ Draw a line under the indefinite pronoun in each sentence.

1. He knows everything about trees.

2. Would anyone like an apple?

3. Someone baked apple pie.

✏️ Write an indefinite pronoun from the Word Bank to complete each sentence.

4. I learned _____ about trees.

5. Has _____ picked apples before?

Lesson 24
READER'S NOTEBOOK

A Tree Is a Plant
Writing: Narrative Writing

Describing Characters

✏️ Write clear details to finish the story.
Some details should describe Rex and Grace.

_____

- -

Rex was a _____ dog. He lived with

_____

- -

a _____ girl named Grace. Grace

_____

- -

liked to sit under the _____ apple

tree in her yard. Grace wanted to teach Rex

_____

- -

to _____ with her. She told Rex

_____

- -

to _____ . When Rex did the trick,

_____

- -

Grace told Rex, "_____ !" Rex wagged

_____

- -

his _____ tail.

Words with *ue, u, u_e*

✏️ Circle the two words in each row that have the same vowel sound.
Write the letters that stand for the sound.

				ue	u	u-e
1.	clue	trust	true	___		___
				- - -		- - -
				___		___
2.	prune	flute	float	___		___
				- - -		- - -
				___		___
3.	goal	flu	truth	___		___
				- - -		- - -
				___		___
4.	tone	tune	rule	___		___
				- - -		- - -
				___		___
5.	blue	blunt	glue	___		___
				- - -		- - -
				___		___

Name _____ Date _____

 Reader's Guide

A Tree Is a Plant

Tree Diagrams

Read pages 136–137. Draw a tree with leaves and roots. Use green arrows to show how food moves. Use blue arrows to show how water moves.

Read pages 128–147. Draw the apple tree in each season. Start with spring. Write the name of each season.

Spelling Words with Vowel Digraphs *oo*, *ou*, *ew*

A Tree Is a Plant
Spelling: Words with *oo*, *ou*, *ew*

✏️ Write each group of Spelling Words in ABC order.

Spelling Words

soon
new
noon
zoo
boot
too
moon
blew
soup
you

soon	moon	too	new
noon	zoo	blew	soup
boot		you	

Indefinite Pronouns

🖉 **Indefinite pronouns** stand for people or things that are not named.

Word Bank

anyone	someone	everyone
something	everybody	everything

🖉 Write an indefinite pronoun from the Word Bank to complete each sentence.

_____

1. We met _____ in the park.

_____

2. Did you bring _____ to eat.

_____

3. Can _____ pick apples with me?

_____

4. I put _____ in the box.

_____

5. _____ likes red apples.

Spelling Words with the *oo* (moon) Sound

A Tree Is a Plant
Spelling: Words with *oo, ou, ew*

✏️ Write the Spelling Word that completes each sentence.

Spelling Words

soon
new
noon
zoo
boot
too
moon
blew
soup
you

_____
- - - - - - - - - - - -
1. We will have our lunch at _____ .

_____
- - - - - - - - - - - -
2. I hope that I will see you _____ .

_____
- - - - - - - - - - - -
3. The wind _____ the tree over.

_____
- - - - - - - - - - - -
4. I saw many animals at the _____ .

_____
- - - - - - - - - - - -
5. There was a full _____ last night.

_____
- - - - - - - - - - - -
6. It is _____ hot to play outside.

_____
- - - - - - - - - - - -
7. We will have _____ for lunch.

_____
- - - - - - - - - - - -
8. I need a _____ pencil.

Spiral Review

Rewrite each sentence to tell about the future.

1. It stopped raining.

_____

- - - - - - - - - - - - - - - - - - -

_____

2. I picked apples.

- - - - - - - - - - - - - - - - - - -

_____

- - - - - - - - - - - - - - - - - - -

_____

3. We learn about trees.

- - - - - - - - - - - - - - - - - - -

_____

4. I climbed a tree.

- - - - - - - - - - - - - - - - - - -

_____

5. They planted new trees.

- - - - - - - - - - - - - - - - - - -

_____

- - - - - - - - - - - - - - - - - - -

_____

Name _____

Planning My Story

 Write and draw details for your story.

Characters	Setting

Plot

Beginning

Middle

End

Grammar in Writing

🖉 Use **indefinite pronouns** to stand for the names of people or things. They do not name certain people or things.

> **Word Bank**
>
> anyone   something   someone
> everything   everyone   everybody

🖉 Write an indefinite pronoun from the Word Bank to complete each sentence.

1. _____ went to the farm.

2. The farmer knew _____ about apples.

3. She helped _____ pick apples.

4. She didn't want _____ to get hurt.

Words with *ou, ow*

 Circle the word that names the picture.

1.

cot   cow

2.

couch   coach

3.

moose   mouse

4.

crow   crown

5.

plate   plow

6.

cloud   closed

Words to Know

✏️ Draw a line to match each picture to the word that goes with it.

1.   **family**

2.   **school**

3.   **party**

4.   **city**

5.   **buy**

6.   **myself**

✏️ Use the words **seven** and **please** together in a sentence. Write it on the line.

_____

- -

_____

Name _____

Words with *ou, ow*

✏️ Circle the word that best completes each sentence.

1. I got a new pet. He's a _____ dog.

    hound   hold

2. He should not jump up on the _____.

    coach   couch

3. At night, my dog _____ at the moon.

    holes   howls

4. My dog's bark is very _____.

    loud   load

5. He will _____ when someone comes to the house!

    grow   growl

6. He sits when I tell him to get _____.

    down   dome

Name _____

Spelling Words with Vowel Diphthongs *ow*, *ou*

✏️ Sort the words. Write the correct Spelling Words in each column.

Words with **ou**	Words with **ow**
_____	_____
_____	_____
_____	_____
_____	_____
_____	_____
_____	_____
_____	_____
_____	_____
_____	_____
_____	_____

Spelling Words

how
now
cow
owl
ouch
house
found
out
gown
town

Name _____

Contractions with *not*

✏️ Write a contraction from the box for the underlined word or words.

Word Bank

isn't

aren't

can't

don't

1. This house <u>is not</u> empty now.

_____

- - - - - - - - - - - - - - - - - - - -

_____

2. I <u>do not</u> know where my books are.

_____

- - - - - - - - - - - - - - - - - - - -

_____

3. They <u>are not</u> in this big box.

_____

- - - - - - - - - - - - - - - - - - - -

_____

4. I <u>cannot</u> find my jump rope.

_____

- - - - - - - - - - - - - - - - - - - -

_____

5. I <u>do not</u> have a new friend yet.

_____

- - - - - - - - - - - - - - - - - - - -

_____

Sentences with Different Lengths

✏️ Make long sentences by joining two short sentences with **and**.

1. Kirk moved to a new city. He was happy.

_____

_____

_____ ,

_____

and _____ .

2. The city is far away. It is very big.

_____

_____

_____ ,

_____

and _____ .

3. Kirk made new friends. He saw new places.

_____

_____

_____ ,

_____

and _____ .

Name _____

Words with *oi, oy, au, aw*

✏️ Circle the two words in each row that have the same vowel sound. Write the letters that stand for the sound.

		oi	oy	au	aw
1.	coins coats join	___	___		
2.	joy boy book	___	___		
3.	house sauce pause	___	___		
4.	dune dawn crawl	___	___	___	
5.	point paint moist	___	___		

Reader's Guide

The New Friend

Meet Makoto!

You get to introduce Makoto to his classmates!

Read pages 166–173. Write three things you know about Makoto. Draw a picture of him.

Read pages 174–181. Makoto wants to bring something to show the class more about his life. Draw a picture to show what he brings. Then write a sentence to tell why he chose it.

_____

_____

_____

_____

The New Friend
Spelling: Words with *ou, ow*

Spelling Words with Vowel Diphthongs *ou*, *ow*

✏️ Write the Spelling Word that fits each clue.

Spelling Words

how
now
cow
owl
ouch
house
found
out
gown
town

1. Opposite of **later** _____

2. Opposite of **lost** _____

3. A farm animal _____

4. Smaller than a city _____

5. Opposite of **in** _____

6. A bird _____

Contractions with Pronouns

 Write a contraction from the box for the underlined words.

Word Bank

I'm   he's   she's   it's

1. It is a pretty day.

_____

- - - - - - - - - - - - - - - - - -

_____

2. I am going to school with my new friend.

_____

- - - - - - - - - - - - - - - - - -

_____

3. He is in the car with his mom.

_____

- - - - - - - - - - - - - - - - - -

_____

4. She is driving us.

_____

- - - - - - - - - - - - - - - - - -

_____

Spelling Words with *ow* and *ou*

✏️ **Write the Spelling Word that completes each sentence.**

Spelling Words

how
house
now
owl
cow
found
town
ouch
out
gown

_____

- - - - - - - - - - - - - - - - - -

1. We're walking to my _____ .

_____

- - - - - - - - - - - - - - - - - -

2. _____ will you get home?

3. Do you live far from

_____

- - - - - - - - - - - - - - - - - -

_____ ?

_____

- - - - - - - - - - - - - - - - - -

4. I'm going _____ to play.

_____

- - - - - - - - - - - - - - - - - -

5. _____ ! That hurt!

_____

- - - - - - - - - - - - - - - - - -

6. He's coming home right _____ .

Spiral Review

✏️ Circle the prepositional phrase in each sentence. Decide if the prepositional phrase tells where or when. Write **where** or **when** on the line.

1. Max and Viv play after school. _____

2. They meet in the park. _____

3. Viv's kite is stuck in a tree. _____

4. They race on the grass. _____

5. The park closes at five o'clock. _____

6. The friends will meet again next week. _____

Grammar in Writing

- A contraction is a short way of writing some words.

- This mark (') takes the place of missing letters.

🖉 **Fix the mistakes in these sentences.**
Use proofreading marks.

Example: ~~H'es~~ He's in a new house.

1. Im' with my new friend.

2. Today shes putting her toys away.

3. She cant' find the games.

4. The books are'nt in the box.

5. We do'nt play today.

Proofreading Marks	
∧	add
⌿	take out

Adding *-ed*, *-ing*

✏ Look at the picture. Read the word.
Circle the **-ed** or **-ing** word that is spelled
correctly.

1. hop	hoping hopeing hopping	
2. bat	batted bated bateed	
3. skate	skating skatting skateing	
4. bike	bikked biked bikeed	
5. hug	huging hugging hugiing	
6. wave	waved waveed wavvd	

Name _____

Words to Know

✏️ Circle the correct word to complete each sentence.

1. A (even, teacher) helps you learn.

2. Please push that box (toward, pushed) me.

3. A (bear, surprised) is a big animal.

4. The lamp is (above, pushed) the shelf.

5. Mom (teacher, pushed) Kim on the swing.

6. Jim was (surprised, even) by his birthday gift.

7. All the family came, (even, above) Grandma.

8. Ben (toward, studied) the painting closely.

Adding -ed, -ing

 Circle the word that fits in the sentence.

1. The cowboy _____ a cow.

   ropped   roped

2. A clown was _____ a red flag.

   waveing   waving

3. The bull _____ running.

   stoped   stopped

4. Kate _____ Silver.

   peted   petted

Spelling Words Ending in *-ed*, *-ing*

✏️ Write the Spelling Words that end in -ing.

_____ _____

1. _____ 2. _____

✏️ Write the Spelling Words that end in -ed.

_____ _____

3. _____ 4. _____

5. _____

✏️ Write the Spelling Words that are base words.

_____ _____

6. _____ 7. _____

8. _____ 9. _____

10. _____

Spelling Words

mix
mixed
hop
hopped
hope
hoping
run
running
use
used

What Is an Exclamation?

 Draw a line under each exclamation.

1. The art show was great!

I saw many paintings.

2. Did you see the painting of the dog?

I liked that one the most!

3. Dee and Jan put the show together.

They did a good job!

4. I hope our class can see that show!

Don't you think so, too?

5. Kay saw the show yesterday.

She wants to see it again!

Showing Strong Feelings

🖉 Finish these sentences that tell your opinion about Vashti's teacher. Write one exclamation that shows a strong feeling.

| Topic Sentence |

_____

I think Vashti's teacher is _____

_____

| Detail Sentence |

_____

I think so because _____

_____

| Detail Sentence |

_____

I also think so because _____

_____

Words with Long *e* Spelling Patterns *y, ie*

✏️ Circle the word that matches the picture. Write the word.

1.

bus   bunny

_____

- - - - - - - - - - - -

_____

2.

park   party

_____

- - - - - - - - - - - -

_____

3.

baby   babies

_____

- - - - - - - - - - - -

_____

4.

chief   cheese

_____

- - - - - - - - - - - -

_____

5.

sunny   seed

_____

- - - - - - - - - - - -

_____

6.

when   windy

_____

- - - - - - - - - - - -

_____

The Dot

Art Awards

Art shows often have awards. The awards are given to the best pieces of art.

Read pages 15–29. Here is an award for the best artwork at the art show.

Which artwork do you think won this award?

_____

- - - - - - - - - - - - - - - - - - -

_____

Why did it win the award?

_____

- - - - - - - - - - - - - - - - - - -

_____

- - - - - - - - - - - - - - - - - - -

_____

- - - - - - - - - - - - - - - - - - -

_____

- - - - - - - - - - - - - - - - - - -

_____

Read pages 30–33. Draw what you think the boy's next artwork will look like. Make an award for it.

Why did it win this award?

_____

- -

_____

- -

_____

Spelling Words Ending in -ed, -ing

✎ **Add -ed to each base word. Then write the new Spelling Word on the line.**

Spelling Words
mix
mixed
hop
hopped
hope
hoping
run
running
use
used

1. mix _____

2. hop _____

3. use _____

✎ **Add -ing to each base word. Then write the new Spelling Word on the line.**

4. hope _____

5. run _____

Writing Exclamations

 Write each sentence as an exclamation.
Begin and end the sentences correctly.

1. those paints are pretty

_____

- - - - - - - - - - - - - - - - - -

_____

2. i love these new pencils

_____

- - - - - - - - - - - - - - - - - -

_____

3. this painting got a prize

_____

- - - - - - - - - - - - - - - - - -

_____

4. there is too much paper

_____

- - - - - - - - - - - - - - - - - -

_____

5. we can't wait to draw

_____

- - - - - - - - - - - - - - - - - -

_____

Planning My Sentences

✏️ **Write your opinion. Then write reasons that tell why. Include a closing sentence.**

My Opinion

First Reason

Second Reason

Closing Sentence

Words with Endings -ed and -ing

 Write the Spelling Word to complete each sentence.

_____
- - - - - - - - - - - - - - - - - - -

1. The bunny _____ away.
(hop, hopped)

_____
- - - - - - - - - - - - - - - - - - -

2. I _____ I will win the race.
(hope, hoping)

_____
- - - - - - - - - - - - - - - - - - -

3. He is _____ very fast.
(run, running)

_____
- - - - - - - - - - - - - - - - - - -

4. Kim _____ all the glue in her art project.
(use, used)

_____
- - - - - - - - - - - - - - - - - - -

5. I _____ the eggs and the butter.
(mix, mixed)

Name _____

Lesson 26
READER'S NOTEBOOK

The Dot
Grammar

Spiral Review

✏️ Circle the pronoun that can take the place of the underlined word or words.

1. <u>Jack and Fred</u> want to paint.

    We   They   He

2. <u>Roy</u> drew a picture of a puppy.

    It   He   She

3. <u>The picture</u> is very big.

    We   It   He

✏️ Write **He, She, It, We,** or **They** to take the place of the underlined word or words.

   _____

4. <u>Jenny</u> went to the art store. _____

   _____

5. <u>Rob and Liz</u> were there. _____

   _____

6. <u>The store</u> is a fun place. _____

Grammar in Writing

An **exclamation** is a sentence that shows strong feeling. It ends with an exclamation point (!).

Example: Meg is an artist.

Revised: Meg is the best artist I know!

Revise each sentence. Make it an exclamation.

1. I like blue.

_____

- - - - - - - - - - - - - - - - - - -

_____

2. Mandy drew a picture.

_____

- - - - - - - - - - - - - - - - - - -

_____

3. Karl likes to paint.

_____

- - - - - - - - - - - - - - - - - - -

_____

4. Your pictures are nice.

_____

- - - - - - - - - - - - - - - - - - -

_____

What Can You Do?
Phonics: Adding *-er*, *-est*
(change *y* to *i*)

Name _____

Adding *-er*, *-est* (change *y* to *i*)

✏️ **Read the words. Circle the word that does not belong.**

1.

fancy | fancier   fanciest   find

2.

happy | happier   hand   happiest

3.

silly | sillier   silliest   still

4.

funny | far   funnier   funniest

5.

jolly | jollier   jolliest   joke

6.

messy | miss   messier   messiest

Name _____

Words to Know

 Circle the best answer to each question.

1. What word goes with **far**? near high

2. What word goes with **plot**? always stories

3. What word goes with **when**? different once

4. What word goes with **just right**? enough near

5. What word goes with **low**? high happy

6. What word goes with **sad**? once happy

7. What word goes with **never**? high always

8. What word goes with **same**? different stories

Name _____

Lesson 27
READER'S NOTEBOOK

What Can You Do?
Phonics: Adding -er, -est
(change y to i)

Adding -er, -est (change y to i)

 Circle the word that best completes the sentence.

1. My glue is _____ .

    sticky   stickier

2. That chick is the _____ of all.

    fluffy   fluffiest

3. This cupcake is _____ .

    yummy   yummiest

4. My hat is the _____ of all.

    fancier   fanciest

5. Her bird makes the _____ sounds.

    sillier   silliest

6. Luke tells _____ jokes.

    funny   funnier

Name _____

Spelling Words Ending in *-er*, *-est*

Sort the words. Write the correct Spelling Words in each column.

Words with **-er**	Words with **-est**
_____	_____
_____	_____
_____	_____
_____	_____
_____	_____
_____	_____

Base Words

_____	_____	_____
_____	_____	_____

Spelling Words

hard
harder
hardest
fast
faster
fastest
slow
slower
slowest
sooner

Question, Exclamation, Statement, or Command?

✏️ Draw a line from each question to the question mark (?). Draw a line from each exclamation to the exclamation point (!). Draw a line from each statement or command to the period(.).

1. I really love to sing

?

!

2. Do you play drums

?

!

3. Give the children a snack

?

.

4. Mark makes the snacks

?

.

5. May I have one

?

.

Write Sentences with *Because*

✏️ Finish these sentences that tell your opinion about learning something new.

Topic Sentence

_____ _____

Learning to _____ is _____ .

hard   easy

Detail Sentence

_____

One reason is _____ .

Detail Sentence

_____

Another reason is _____ .

Closing Sentence

_____ _____

Learning to _____ is _____ .

Syllable *-le*

 Circle the word that names the picture.

1.

bottle   bubble

2.

handle   candle

3.

paddle   apple

4.

circle   cattle

5.

bumble   beetle

6.

poodle   puzzle

Reader's Guide

What Can You Do?

Lessons to Learn

The selection has important lessons about practicing, trying hard, and learning new things.

Read pages 51–59. What did you learn about practicing?

_____

- -

_____

_____

- -

_____

_____

- -

_____

_____

- -

_____

Read pages 60–69. What is the moral or lesson of the whole selection?

_____

- -

_____

_____

- -

_____

Think of two animal characters who
have a problem they can fix by practicing.
List the characters and the setting. Tell what
happens first, next, and last. Then write your
story on another sheet of paper.

My Characters	My Setting

Events in My Story

Spelling Words Ending in *-er*, *-est*

✏️ **Add -er to each base word. Then write the new Spelling Word on the line.**

Spelling Words

hard
harder
hardest
fast
faster
fastest
slow
slower
slowest
sooner

1. hard _____

2. fast _____

3. slow _____

4. soon _____

✏️ **Add -est to each base word. Then write the Spelling Word on the line.**

5. hard _____

6. fast _____

7. slow _____

Kinds of Sentences

 Combine the two shorter sentences to write a compound sentence.

1. Go home. Come with us.

_____

_____ , or _____

2. Dan loves to run! He loves to swim even more!

_____ , but

_____

_____

3. I can knit. I can sew.

_____ , and _____

_____

4. Will Jen come home soon? Will she be out late?

_____ , or

_____

_____

Planning My Sentences

 Write your opinion. Then write reasons that tell why.

My Opinion

First Reason

Second Reason

Closing Sentence

Words with Endings
-er and *-est*

✏️ Write the Spelling Word that completes each sentence.

fast　　　　faster　　　　fastest

_____

1. The bus goes _____ .

_____

2. The truck goes _____ than the bus.

_____

3. The car goes the _____ .

slow　　　　slower　　　　slowest

_____

4. The bug is _____ .

_____

5. The worm is _____ than the bug.

_____

6. The turtle is the _____ of all.

Spiral Review

 Choose the correct words from the word box to finish each sentence.

Mark	I	me

_____ _____

1. _____ and _____ act in a play.

I	Tammy	me

_____ _____

2. The teacher reads _____ and _____ a story.

me	I	Ricky

_____ _____

3. Nana watches _____ and _____ .

I	me	Sue

_____ _____

4. _____ and _____ like to slide.

Grammar in Writing

A **statement** and a **command** end with a period. A **question** ends with a question mark. An **exclamation** ends with an exclamation point. All sentences begin with capital letters.

Revise each sentence. Change it to the kind shown in ( ).

> Example: Glen can read. (question)
> Can Glen read?

1. Is skating fun? (statement)

_____

- - - - - - - - - - - - - - - - - -

_____

2. I like to ride my bike. (exclamation)

_____

- - - - - - - - - - - - - - - - - -

_____

3. Chuck likes to act. (question)

_____

- - - - - - - - - - - - - - - - - -

_____

4. You write a story. (command)

_____

- - - - - - - - - - - - - - - - - -

_____

Long *i* Spelling Patterns *igh, y, ie*

Look at the picture. Circle the word that names the picture.

1.

   spy   line

2.

   pine   pie

3.

   sky   nine

4.

   high   hive

5.

   think   thigh

6.

   fine   fly

Words to Know

 Circle the correct word in each sentence.

1. The cat plays with a (ball, head) of yarn.

2. We all (cried, heard) the crash.

3. You (heard, should) try these grapes.

4. Jean is the (second, ball) girl in line.

5. "Let's go!" (cried, heard) Kenny.

6. My (large, head) hurts.

7. We are running (second, across) the field.

8. There is a (large, heard) bird in the tree.

183

Name _____

Long *i* Spelling Patterns *igh*, *y*, *ie*

 Write a word from the box to finish each sentence.

thigh	dry	try	tie	high

_____

- - - - - - - - - - - - - - - -

1. Sam hurt his _____ when he fell.

_____

- - - - - - - - - - - - - - -

2. Dad's _____ has dots and stripes.

_____

- - - - - - - - - - - - - -

3. I will _____ to swim.

_____

- - - - - - - - - - - - - - -

4. The bird will fly up _____.

_____

- - - - - - - - - - - - - - -

5. The wet shirt will _____.

Spelling Words with Patterns *igh*, *y*, *ie*

🖉 Write the Spelling Words with the **igh** pattern.

_____   _____

1. _____   2. _____

🖉 Write the Spelling Words with the **ie** pattern.

_____   _____

3. _____   4. _____

🖉 Write the Spelling Words with the **y** spelling.

_____   _____

5. _____   6. _____

7. _____   8. _____

9. _____   10. _____

Spelling Words

my

try

sky

fly

by

dry

pie

cried

night

light

Name _____

Adjectives for Taste and Smell

 Draw a line under each adjective.
Then write the adjective.

1. I smell the sweet roses.

   _____

   - - - - - - - - - - - - - - - -

   _____

2. We taste the bitter lemon.

   _____

   - - - - - - - - - - - - - - - -

   _____

3. Does the milk smell sour?

   _____

   - - - - - - - - - - - - - - - -

   _____

 Draw a line under each adjective and
add commas where they are needed.

4. Some nuts are crunchy sweet and salty.

5. The fruit was sweet moist and chewy.

Using Different Words

Change a repeated word to an exact
word. Use a word from the box or your own.

bright	down	high
flew	funny	blue
mean	ran	sunny

Toad <u>went</u> fast, and the kite <u>went</u> up.

_____

Toad _____ fast, and the kite went up.

The <u>little</u> birds laughed at Toad's <u>little</u> kite.

_____

The little birds laughed at Toad's _____ kite.

The <u>pretty</u> kite danced in the <u>pretty</u> sky.

_____

The pretty kite danced in the _____ sky.

Adding -ed, -ing, -er, -est, -es

✏️ Write the word that best completes each sentence. Use words from the box.

| smaller | jumped | riding | highest | foxes |

_____

1. Those trees are the _____ of all.

_____

2. That bird is _____ than this one.

_____

3. Who is _____ a red bike?

_____

4. A frog _____ into the pond.

_____

5. Five _____ ran to the woods.

Name _____   Date _____

The Kite

Frog, Toad, and the Robins

Read pages 88–93. The robins made fun
of the kite. Now draw a cartoon. Draw
Frog. Make a speech bubble to show what he
says to the robins.

Read pages 94–101. Now draw a cartoon. Show what Frog might say to the robins at the end of the story.

Spelling Words with Patterns *igh*, *y*, *ie*

✏️ Write each group of Spelling Words in ABC order.

my	try	dry	pie
sky	fly	cried	night
by		light	

_____	_____
_____	_____
_____	_____
_____	_____
_____	_____
_____	_____

Spelling Words

my

try

sky

fly

by

dry

pie

cried

night

light

Adjectives for Sound and Texture

 Draw a line under each adjective.
Then write the adjective.

1. We sail on the smooth lake.

_____

- - - - - - - - - - - - - - - - - -

_____

2. I hear the loud cry of a seagull.

_____

- - - - - - - - - - - - - - - - - -

_____

3. The blanket feels warm.

_____

- - - - - - - - - - - - - - - - - -

_____

✏️ Draw a line under each adjective and
add commas where they are needed.

4. The beat was noisy loud and pounding.

5. The music was soft catchy and nice.

Planning My Sentences

✏️ Write your opinion. Then write reasons that tell why. Include a closing sentence.

My Opinion

First Reason

Second Reason

Closing Sentence

Name _____

Spelling Words with *igh*, *y*, *ie*

✏️ Write the correct word to complete each sentence.

_____

_ _ _ _ _ _ _ _ _ _ _ _ _ _ _ _

1. Please turn on the _____ .

    (cried, light, pie)

_____

_ _ _ _ _ _ _ _ _ _ _ _ _ _ _ _

2. Have you seen _____ book?

    (my, try, night)

_____

_ _ _ _ _ _ _ _ _ _ _ _ _ _ _ _

3. The baby _____ in her crib.

    (fly, dry, cried)

_____

_ _ _ _ _ _ _ _ _ _ _ _ _ _ _ _

4. Make sure to _____ the dishes.

    (dry, my, light)

_____

_ _ _ _ _ _ _ _ _ _ _ _ _ _ _ _

5. We went to a great play last _____ .

    (light, night, fly)

Spiral Review

 Write the correct pronoun to finish each sentence.

1. Is the yellow kite _____ ?

your   yours

2. That is _____ kite.

her   hers

3. Rex put away _____ kite.

he   his

4. Would you like to play at _____ house?

my   mine

5. We went to _____ party.

their   theirs

Grammar in Writing

Some adjectives describe nouns by telling about **taste**, **smell**, **sound**, or **feel**.

Example: I feel the ^cool breeze.

🖊 **Revise each sentence. Use the proofreading mark to add an adjective.**

sweet	fresh	happy	soft

1. Mr. Bee shares some honey.

2. The frog gave a croak.

3. We sit on the grass.

4. We enjoy the air.

Proofreading Mark	
∧	add

196

Suffixes *-ful*, *-ly*, *-y*

 Write a suffix from the box to finish the word.

ful	ly	y

1.

sad _____

2.

bump _____

3.

dust _____

4.

help _____

5.

slow _____

6.

safe _____

Words to Know

 Circle the correct word to complete each sentence.

1. Planting vegetables is a good (minute, idea).

2. Juan (caught, listen) the ball.

3. Mom (took, caught) us for a haircut.

4. Nancy (idea, thought) about what to bake.

5. My sister has a (beautiful, friendship) new bike.

6. Please (listen, took) to the teacher.

7. My cousin will be here in a (minute, listen).

8. My (beautiful, friendship) with Rita is important to me.

198

Name _____

Suffixes -*ful*, -*ly*, -*y*

Choose a word from the box. Choose a suffix to make a new word. Write the new word below the suffix.

spoon	snow	sad	trick	
joy	quick	peace	dirt	glad

y	ly	ful

Name _____

Spelling Words with the Suffixes *-ly*, *-y*, *-ful*

Write the Spelling Words with -ly.

1. _____ 2. _____

Write the Spelling Words with -y.

3. _____ 4. _____

Write the Spelling Word with -ful.

5. _____

Write the Spelling Words that are base words.

6. _____ 7. _____

8. _____ 9. _____

10. _____

Spelling Words

sad
sadly
slow
slowly
dust
dusty
trick
tricky
help
helpful

Adverbs for How and Where

 Circle the adverb in each sentence.
Write it on the line.

_____

_____

1. The man went upstairs.   _____

_____

2. The dog followed him closely.   _____

_____

3. Buzz is here.   _____

_____

4. He watched the fly carefully.   _____

Complete each sentence. Write an adverb
that tells how or where.

_____

5. The leaf floated _____ down the stream.

_____

6. Jose stores his new boat _____ .

Lesson 29
READER'S NOTEBOOK

Hi! Fly Guy
Writing: Opinion Writing

Giving Examples

✏️ Look at the picture of the judges on page 139 of your book. Write your opinion about how the judges are feeling about their decision.

_____

- - - - - - - - - - - - - - - - - -

I think the judges are feeling _____.

✏️ Write one reason to explain your opinion.

_____

- - - - - - - - - - - - - - - - - -

One reason is _____

✏️ Write two examples to explain your reason.

_____

- - - - - - - - - - - - - - - - - -

1. _____

- - - - - - - - - - - - - - - - - -

_____

- - - - - - - - - - - - - - - - - -

_____

- - - - - - - - - - - - - - - - - -

2. _____

- - - - - - - - - - - - - - - - - -

_____

- - - - - - - - - - - - - - - - - -

Name _____

Lesson 29
READER'S NOTEBOOK

Hi! Fly Guy
Phonics: Long Vowel Spelling
Patterns: *a, e, i, o, u*

Long Vowel Spelling Patterns *a, e, i, o, u*

✏️ Circle the two words in each row that rhyme. Then write the letter that spells the long vowel sound.

1.

table   hi   fable   me

_____

2.

hi   she   he   go

_____

3.

kind   no   flu   mind

_____

4.

flu   Stu   so   be

_____

5.

we   hold   wind   told

_____

Hi! Fly Guy

Fly Talk

You have a special machine.
It tells you what Fly says!

Read pages 119–125. Use your imagination! What does
Fly Guy mean when he says "Buzz!" on page 124?

Read pages 126–128. What does Fly Guy mean when he
says "Buzz!" on page 128?

Read pages 129–130. **What does Fly Guy mean when he says "Buzz!" on page 130?**

Buzz! →

_____

_____

- - - - - - - - - - - - - - - - - -

_____

- - - - - - - - - - - - - - - - - -

_____

- - - - - - - - - - - - - - - - - -

Read pages 131–141. **What does Fly Guy mean when he says "Buzz!" on page 136?**

Buzz! →

_____

- - - - - - - - - - - - - - - - - -

_____

- - - - - - - - - - - - - - - - - -

_____

- - - - - - - - - - - - - - - - - -

Spelling Words with the Suffixes *-ly, -y, -ful*

Spelling Words

sad
sadly
slow
slowly
dust
dusty
trick
tricky
help
helpful

Add -ly to each base word. Then write the new Spelling Word on the line.

_____

1. sad

_____

2. slow

Add -y to each base word. Then write the new Spelling Word on the line.

_____

3. dust

_____

4. trick

Add -ful to the base word. Then write the new Spelling Word on the line.

_____

5. help

Adverbs for When and How Much

✏️ Circle the adverb in each sentence. Write it on the line.

_____

1. The wagon is too heavy to pull. _____

2. Dwayne arrived late to the picnic. _____

3. He was very happy to see his friends. _____

4. They will have a ball game soon. _____

✏️ Complete each sentence. Write an adverb that tells when or how much.

_____

5. We will have a pet show _____.

6. The bucket was _____ full.

Words with the Suffixes -*ly*, -*y*, -*ful*

Write the correct word from the box to complete each sentence.

1. I did a card _____ .

trick
tricky

2. It was _____ to find the
way to the park.

trick
tricky

3. I like to _____ wash
the car.

help
helpful

4. When I wash the car, I am very

_____ .

help
helpful

5. I was _____ to hear my
mom call me home.

sad
sadly

6. I _____ walked home.

sad
sadly

Spiral Review

Indefinite pronouns stand for the names of people or things. They do not take the place of a noun for a certain person or thing, though.

✏ Write the indefinite pronoun that best completes the sentence.

_____
- -

1. Fly Guy knew _____ about being a pet.

   something   anyone

_____
- -

2. Buzz liked _____ about Fly Guy.

   everyone   everything

_____
- -

3. _____ was amazed by Fly Guy.

   Everyone   Everything

_____
- -

4. Did _____ teach Fly Guy his tricks?

   everything   someone

Planning My Opinion Paragraph

Write your opinion. Write reasons and examples. Then write a closing sentence.

My Opinion

First Reason
Example

Second Reason
Example

Closing Sentence

Grammar in Writing

Adverbs can tell **how**, **where**, **when**,
or **how much**.

Examples:	Buzz ran <u>quickly</u>.	how
	Buzz ran <u>here</u>.	where
	Buzz ran <u>yesterday</u>.	when
	Buzz ran <u>a lot</u>.	how much

Rewrite each sentence. Add the kind of
adverb shown in ( ).

1. Flies find food. (where)

_____

- -

_____

2. Fly Guy chewed a leaf. (when)

_____

- -

_____

3. He chewed. (how)

_____

- -

_____

4. He ate. (how much)

_____

- -

_____

Syllable Pattern CV

✏️ Read each word. Draw a line to divide the CV word into two syllables.

1.

music   might

2.

baby   bone

3.

lace   lady

4.

part   pilot

5.

robber   robot

6.

motel   miss

Name _____

Words to Know

 Circle the best answer to each clue.

1. This means **all people.**   everyone   field

2. This means **liked a lot.**   most   loved

3. These are children and adults.   sorry   people

4. **Sisters** is its opposite.   brothers   loved

5. This is a place to play soccer.   most   field

6. This means **almost all.**   people   most

7. This means **a certain number.**   field   only

8. This is **a kind of feeling.**   sorry   everyone

Syllable Pattern CV

✏️ In each sentence, circle the CV word that has two syllables.

1. It is a bright, shiny day!

2. There is a huge hotel by the lake.

3. Big boats sail in the wavy tide.

4. I hope you decide to come see me.

5. We could take a slow, lazy ride on a boat.

Spelling Words with CV Syllables

Write the Spelling Words with the long e sound in the first syllable.

_____   _____

1. _____   2. _____

_____   _____

3. _____   4. _____

Write the Spelling Words with the long a sound in the first syllable.

_____   _____

5. _____   6. _____

_____

7. _____

Write the Spelling Words with these long vowel sounds in the first syllable.

_____   _____

8. long **i** _____   9. long **o** _____

_____

10. long **u** _____

Spelling Words

even
open
begin
baby
tiger
music
paper
zero
table
below

Adjectives with *er* and *est*

✏️ Circle the correct adjective to finish each sentence. Write the adjective.

_____

- - - - - - - - - - - - - - - - - -

1. Tim is _____ than Max.

taller   tallest

_____

- - - - - - - - - - - - - - - - - -

2. Fred is the _____ of them all.

taller   tallest

_____

- - - - - - - - - - - - - - - - - -

3. Cathy is _____ than Cam.

older   oldest

_____

- - - - - - - - - - - - - - - - - -

4. Adam is the _____ player of all.

smaller   smallest

Writing a Closing Sentence

✏️ Do you think Mia should have quit? Write your own words that explain your opinion. Listen to the words in the Word Bank. Read along. Be sure your last sentence retells your opinion.

Word Bank

| agree | disagree | decision | reason | example |

_____

_____

I _____ with Mia's decision to

_____

quit. One reason is _____ .

_____

For example, _____ .

_____

Another reason is _____ .

_____

_____

I think _____ .

Prefixes *un-*, *re-*

 Read each word. Circle the word in each box that matches the picture.

1.

untie   tried

2.

read   repaint

3.

setting   remove

4.

bedding   unbraid

5.

untidy   neat

6.

unzip   unbutton

Winners Never Quit!

Soccer Stories

You just read about Mia Hamm, a famous soccer player. How do you think her brother and sister would tell the story?

Read pages 159–167. How do you think Lovdy would tell this part of the story?

_____

- - - - - - - - - - - - - - - - - - -

_____

- - - - - - - - - - - - - - - - - - -

_____

- - - - - - - - - - - - - - - - - - -

_____

- - - - - - - - - - - - - - - - - - -

_____

- - - - - - - - - - - - - - - - - - -

_____

- - - - - - - - - - - - - - - - - - -

_____

Read pages 168–177. How do you think Garrett would tell this part of the story?

_____

- -

_____

- -

_____

- -

_____

- -

_____

- -

_____

- -

_____

Do you think Mia scored at the end? What do you think Lovdy and Garrett said to her?

_____

- -

_____

- -

_____

- -

_____

Spelling Words with CV Syllables

Winners Never Quit!
Spelling: Words with
CV Syllables

✏️ Write the Spelling Word that fits
each clue.

Spelling Words

even
open
begin
baby
tiger
music
paper
zero
table
below

1. Opposite of **closed**   _____

2. A very young person   _____

3. Something to listen to   _____

4. Opposite of **end**   _____

5. Opposite of **above**   _____

6. An animal   _____

Using the Right Adjective

✏️ Write adjectives from the Word Banks to finish the sentences.

Word Bank

green   greener   greenest

_____

1. Our yard is _____ .

_____

2. Your yard is _____ than ours.

_____

3. His yard is the _____ of all.

Word Bank

long   longer   longest

_____

4. We played a _____ game today.

_____

5. The game yesterday was _____ than the game today.

Name _____

Lesson 30
READER'S NOTEBOOK

Winners Never Quit!
Spelling: Words with
Syllable Pattern CV

Spelling Words with Syllable Pattern CV

✏️ Write the correct word to complete each sentence.

_____

- - - - - - - - - - - - - - - - - - -

1. Ken saw a _____ at the zoo.
(below, tiger)

_____

- - - - - - - - - - - - - - - - - - -

2. Please sit and _____ your test.
(even, begin)

_____

- - - - - - - - - - - - - - - - - - -

3. What kind of _____ do you like?
(below, music)

_____

- - - - - - - - - - - - - - - - - - -

4. I used red _____ to make the card.
(paper, zero)

_____

- - - - - - - - - - - - - - - - - - -

5. The food is on the _____ .
(open, table)

Name _____

Spiral Review

✏️ Choose contractions from the box for the underlined words. Write the contractions.

1. <u>They are</u> tennis players.

_____

- - - - - - - - - - - - - - - - -

_____

Word Bank

He's

I'm

can't

They're

isn't

2. I <u>cannot</u> wait to play with her.

_____

- - - - - - - - - - - - - - - - -

_____

3. It <u>is not</u> hard to play.

_____

- - - - - - - - - - - - - - - - -

_____

4. <u>He is</u> learning now!

_____

- - - - - - - - - - - - - - - - -

_____

5. <u>I am</u> having fun.

_____

- - - - - - - - - - - - - - - - -

_____

Grammar in Writing

- Add **er** to adjectives to compare two.
- Add **est** to compare more than two.

    Example: Today is warm.

    Today is the warmest day of the summer.

✏️ **Revise each sentence. Use an adjective that compares. Add other words, too.**

1. Beth is a fast runner.

_____

- -

_____

2. Tad is tall.

_____

- -

_____

3. Our team is stronger.

_____

- -

_____

4. Today was cold.

_____

- -

_____

Name _____ Date _____

Unit 6
READER'S NOTEBOOK
Owl at Home
Segment 1
Independent Reading

Reader's Guide

Owl at Home

Case of the Messy Houseguest

Read pages 5–17. Owl thinks Winter
came into his house and made a
big mess. Is he right?

Write in the detective journal. What do you
think really happened? Use clues from the
text and pictures to explain your answer.

_____
- -
_____
- -
_____
_____
_____
- -
_____
_____
_____
- -
_____

Name _____ Date _____

Unit 6
READER'S NOTEBOOK

Owl at Home
Segment 1
Independent Reading

Case of the Mysterious Bumps

Read pages 19–29. There are two bumps at the bottom of Owl's bed. What are they?

Use your detective skills to solve the mystery! Write what you think the bumps are. Use clues from the text and pictures to explain your answer.

_____

_____

_____

_____

_____

_____

_____

_____

_____

_____

_____

Name _____ Date _____

Unit 6
READER'S NOTEBOOK

Owl at Home
Segment 2
Independent Reading

Owl at Home

Case of the Tear-Water Tea

Read pages 31–39. Owl makes
salty tea. Why is the tea salty?

Write in the detective journal. Tell why
the tea is salty. Use clues from the text
and pictures to explain your answer.

Name _____ Date _____

Unit 6
READER'S NOTEBOOK

Owl at Home
Segment 2
Independent Reading

Case of the Upstairs and Downstairs

Read pages 41–49. Help Owl understand why he cannot be upstairs and downstairs at the same time.

Use clues from the story to explain. Draw a picture and label it to solve the mystery for Owl.

Name _____ Date _____

Unit 6
READER'S NOTEBOOK

Owl at Home
Segment 3
Independent Reading

Reader's Guide

Owl at Home

Case of the Moon Friend

Read pages 51–64. Owl looks at
the moon and thinks it is a friend.
Can the moon be Owl's friend?

Write your answer. Use clues from the text
and pictures to explain.

_____

- -

_____

- -

_____

- -

_____

- -

_____

- -

_____

- -

_____

Meet Owl

Use what you know about
Owl to help him build a webpage.
First, draw a picture of Owl in
the box. Then fill in the blanks.

My Name: _____

_____

I live in _____.

My favorite place is _____.

My favorite drink is _____.

My favorite thing to do is _____.

Right now, you can find me _____.

231

Reading and Writing Glossary

Use this glossary to help you remember and use words that you are learning about reading and writing.

A

....

adjective A word that describes a person, an animal, a place, or a thing. An adjective may tell how something looks, tastes, smells, sounds, or feels.

adverb A word that describes a verb. An adverb may tell how, where, when, or how much something is. An adverb may end in *-ly*.

alphabetical order When words are listed in the same order as letters of the alphabet.

antonym A word that means the opposite or nearly the opposite of another word.

apostrophe A punctuation mark (') that takes the place of missing letters in a word.

article A special word, such as *a*, *an*, or *the*, that comes before a noun.

author A person who writes a story.

author's purpose The reason why an author writes a text.

B

base word A word to which beginning and ending word parts can be added. A base word is also known as a root word.

biography Informational text that tells about events in a real person's life.

C

caption Words that tell about a picture or a photograph.

categorize To name a group of similar things.

category A group of like objects or things.

cause The reason why something happens in a story or text.

chapter book A story that is divided into parts.

characteristic A special quality or trait.

characters The people and animals in a story.

checklist A list of names or things to think about or do.

classify To place similar things in a group.

command A sentence that tells someone to do something. A command can end with a period (.) or an exclamation mark (!).

compare To tell how things are the same.

compound sentence A sentence that is made up of two shorter sentences. The parts of a compound sentence may be connected by words such as *and*, *or*, and *but*.

conclusion A good guess about something the author does not say.

context The words and sentences around a word or phrase that give readers clues to its meaning.

contraction A short way of writing two words using an apostrophe (').

contrast To tell how things are different.

D

detail A fact that tells more about the main idea.

dialogue What characters say in a story.

E

effect The result of something that happens in a story or text.

entry word A word listed in a dictionary with a definition.

event Something that happens.

exclamation A sentence that shows a strong feeling. An exclamation begins with a capital letter and ends with an exclamation point (!).

F

fable A short story that teaches a lesson.

fairy tale An old story with characters that can do amazing things.

fantasy A type of story that could not happen in real life.

figurative language Words authors use to help a reader picture things in a story. These words may have more than one meaning.

folktale An old story that people have told for many years.

G

glossary A list of words with their definitions, often at the back of a book.

graph A drawing that uses numbers, colors, pictures, or symbols to give information.

graphic features Photos or drawings that stand for ideas or add details in the text.

H

heading A title for a section of a text.

homograph A word that is spelled the same as another word but has a different meaning and may be pronounced differently.

homophone A word that sounds like another word but is spelled differently and has a different meaning.

I

indefinite pronoun A special pronoun, like *anyone*, *everything*, *someone*, *something*, or *everyone*. An indefinite pronoun does not stand for a certain person or thing.

informational text Text that tells about things that are real and contains facts.

informative writing Writing that gives facts about a topic.

M

....

main idea The most important idea about the topic.

multiple-meaning word A word with more than one meaning.

N

....

narrative nonfiction A story that gives information about real people, settings, and events.

narrative writing Writing that tells a story. A narrative tells about something that happened to a person or a character.

narrator The person who tells the story.

noun A word that names a person, an animal, a place, or a thing.

O

onomatopoeia Using words that sound like real noises.

opinion writing Writing that tells what the writer believes and gives reasons.

P

plot The order of events in a story, including the problem and how it is solved.

plural noun A noun that names more than one person, animal, place, or thing. A plural noun usually ends in -s or -es.

poetry Uses the sounds of words to show pictures and feelings. Poetry sometimes uses rhyming words and other patterns.

possessive noun A noun that shows that one person or animal owns or has something.

possessive pronouns A type of pronoun that shows that something belongs to someone.

predicate The part of a sentence that tells what someone or something does.

prefix A word part attached to the beginning of a base word or root word that changes the word's meaning.

preposition A word that joins with other words to help explain where something is or when it happens.

prepositional phrase A group of words that starts with a preposition.

proper noun A noun that names a special person, animal, place, or thing. A proper noun begins with a capital letter.

Q

question A sentence that asks something. A question begins with a capital letter and ends with a question mark (?).

quotation marks Punctuation marks (" ") that go around the words a character says.

R

realistic fiction A made-up story that could happen in real life.

repetition The same words or same kind of event used over and over in a text.

research report Writing that tells what a writer learned from doing research about a topic.

rhythm A pattern of beats in a poem.

S

sentence A group of words that tells a complete idea.

sequence of events The order in which things happen.

setting When and where a story takes place.

simile Words that tell how two things are the same, using *like* or *as*.

singular noun A noun that names one person, animal, place, or thing.

statement A sentence that tells something. A statement begins with a capital letter and ends with a period (.).

story lesson The lesson a story teaches or its main message.

subject The part of a sentence that tells who or what.

subject pronoun A word that can take the place of a subject, such as *he*, *she*, *it*, *we*, or *they*.

suffix One or more letters that are added to the end of a root word to change the word's meaning.

synonym A word that has the same or almost the same meaning as another word.

T

text and graphic features Photographs, labels, headings, captions, illustrations, dark print, and other special features that add information to a text.

text evidence Clues in the words and pictures that help you figure things out.

thesaurus A book of words in alphabetical order with their synonyms.

topic What a text is mostly about.

V

verb A word that tells what people and animals do.

W

word choice Words writers choose to make their writing clear and interesting, such as words that describe how things look, feel, sound, smell, or taste.